LAUGHING AT ADULTING

A COMICAL BOOK TO LIFE'S ABSURDITIES

STRUCTURE OF THE BOOK

In today's world, there are several topics and aspects of life that people often find challenging and frustrating, contributing to feelings of craziness. Here's a list of such topics:

1. Technology Overload: Constant connectivity and the pressure to be active on multiple social media platforms can be overwhelming.

2. Health and Wellness: Navigating healthcare systems, maintaining physical and mental health, and the inundation of often contradictory health advice online.

3. Work-Life Balance: Juggling a career and personal life, especially with the rise of remote work and the blurring lines between work and home life.

4. Environmental Concerns: Worrying about climate change, sustainability, and the future of the planet can be a source of anxiety.

5. Economic Pressures: Rising costs of living, job security, and financial planning for the future are major stressors.

6. Political Polarization: The intensity and divisiveness of current political climates in many countries can lead to significant stress and frustration.

7. Social Isolation: Despite being more connected than ever digitally, many people feel a sense of loneliness and disconnection from real-life communities.

8. Education and Parenting: Concerns over education quality, parenting challenges, and the pressures faced by both students and parents in the modern education system.

9. Cultural Shifts: Rapid changes in social norms, cultural values, and the pace of life can lead to a sense of disconnection or nostalgia for simpler times.

10. Personal Identity and Self-Expression: Struggles with self-identity, societal expectations, and the freedom to express oneself authentically.

11. Future Uncertainty: Concerns about personal and global future, driven by rapid technological advancements and changing societal structures.

12. Information Overload: The constant barrage of news, information, and content from various sources can be mentally exhausting.

Addressing these topics in your book with humor and empathy can make it very relatable and engaging for a wide audience.

1.

TECHNOLOGY OVERLOAD

Woke up to 47 notifications.
My phone is more popular
than I am before breakfast.

MY SMARTWATCH CONGRATULATED ME ON A GOOD
NIGHT'S SLEEP.
FINALLY, THE RECOGNITION I DESERVE.

In the symphony of digital beeps,
finding the mute button is the true
morning miracle.

START YOUR DAY ON YOUR TERMS,
NOT YOUR NOTIFICATIONS'.
REMEMBER, EVEN THE SUN DOESN'T
RUSH TO RISE.

LOST AN HOUR ON SOCIAL MEDIA, FOUND MY SECOND COUSIN'S CAT'S INSTAGRAM. IT WAS A PURR-FECT WASTE OF TIME.

Social media: where I'm an influencer in the vast kingdom of my 47 followers.

SCROLLING THROUGH LIFE ONE THUMB SWIPE AT A TIME.

DIVE DEEP INTO REAL CONNECTIONS; SHALLOW WATERS ARE FOR SCREENS.

Emails multiply faster than rabbits. I'm considering an inbox spay and neuter program.

MY EMAIL'S FAVORITE HOBBY: SYNCHRONIZING. IT'S ALWAYS SYNCING, BUT NEVER SWIMMING.

Facing an inbox is like opening a door to Narnia, but instead of adventure, it's just more emails.

TACKLE YOUR INBOX WITH THE COURAGE OF A KNIGHT AND THE STRATEGY OF A CHESS MASTER. CHECKMATE, NOT CHECK MAIL.

My gadgets have started forming their own ecosystem. I'm just living in it.

I HAVE MORE CHARGING CABLES THAN FRIENDS. THEY'RE LESS ELECTRIFYING, THOUGH.

IN THE KINGDOM OF GADGETS, THE ONE WITH THE LONGEST BATTERY LIFE RULES.

SIMPLIFY YOUR DIGITAL LIFE; LET'S NOT BE OUTSMARTED BY OUR SMARTPHONES.

Passwords are like pet names, but less affectionate and more forgettable.

CHANGED ALL MY PASSWORDS TO 'INCORRECT.' NOW MY COMPUTER JUST TELLS ME WHEN I FORGET.

Passwords: the modern-day magic spells where forgetting a letter curses you to the realm of 'reset your password'.

Create a password as strong as your coffee and as memorable as your first crush.

I've got more apps than a five-course meal. Still hungry for more.

THERE'S AN APP FOR EVERYTHING. EXCEPT, MAYBE, HOW TO LIVE WITHOUT AN APP FOR EVERYTHING.

Apps are like digital marshmallows. Too many, and you're stuck in a sticky situation.

Balance your app-etite; feast on life's real treats.

My watchlist is so long, I'll need another lifetime. Accepting reincarnation theories now.

BINGE-WATCHING SHOWS IS MY CARDIO. MY THUMB IS IN GREAT SHAPE.

IN THE MARATHON OF STREAMING, MY COUCH AND I ARE GOING FOR GOLD.

Stream your dreams, but don't let them streamroll your reality. There's more to life than the next episode.

2.

HEALTH AND WELLNESS

I joined a gym and they asked my goals.
'To stop coming here by March' seemed honest enough.

MY FAVORITE WORKOUT MACHINE AT THE GYM IS THE VENDING MACHINE.

Joining a gym is the adult version of 'The dog ate my homework.'

EMBRACE YOUR FITNESS JOURNEY, EVEN IF IT OCCASIONALLY DETOURS THROUGH THE DRIVE-THRU.

MY DIET PLAN IS SIMPLE: IF I CAN'T PRONOUNCE IT, I CAN'T EAT IT. QUINOA'S STILL A MYSTERY.

I'm on a seafood diet. I see food, and I eat it.

Dieting is wishing for a thinner body but buttering both sides of the toast just in case.

BALANCE IS KEY IN DIETING. REMEMBER, EVEN LIFE IS TASTELESS WITHOUT A LITTLE SUGAR AND SPICE.

Downloaded a meditation app. It keeps sending 'relax' notifications. Now, I have notification anxiety.

WELLNESS APPS REMIND ME OF EXES. THEY NOTICE WHEN YOU'RE NOT PAYING ATTENTION.

Wellness apps: because what's better than having a tiny coach in your pocket that's judgier than your mom?

Let wellness apps guide, not govern, your journey to health.
Your best coach is your own body.

MEDITATION ADVICE: 'FOCUS ON YOUR BREATH.' ME: 'DID I LEAVE THE STOVE ON?

Tried meditating. Ended up taking a nap. Same thing, right?

Meditation: because sometimes, the best answers come when you forget the questions.

IN THE SILENCE OF MEDITATION, LET YOUR MIND WANDER. IT KNOWS THE WAY BACK.

BOUGHT AN AVOCADO.
IT WAS HARD AS A ROCK FOR A WEEK AND RIPE FOR EXACTLY 7 MINUTES.

Superfoods are like superheroes. They come in bright colors and promise to save the world.

SUPERFOODS: SPENDING MORE TIME BEING PHOTOGRAPHED THAN ACTUALLY BEING EATEN.

Nourish your body with care, but don't forget to treat it sometimes. Happiness is also a superfood.

They say, 'You can sleep when you're dead.'
Pretty sure I'll be up late worrying about that too.

SLEEP IS LIKE A SOFTWARE UPDATE FOR YOUR BRAIN. MINE KEEPS FAILING AT 25%.

Sleep: that elusive state between coffee and internet.

CHERISH YOUR SLEEP; IT'S THE NIGHTLY REBOOT YOUR BODY AND MIND DESPERATELY CRAVE.

Went for crystal healing. Left with glitter that I'm still finding on me weeks later.

TRIED HOLISTIC REMEDIES. NOT SURE IF I'M CURED, BUT I SMELL LIKE A GARDEN.

Alternative therapies: where 'feeling different' is half the cure.

EXPLORE WELLNESS BEYOND THE NORM. HEALING COMES IN MANY FORMS, INCLUDING LAUGHTER.

3.

WORK-LIFE BALANCE

My living room has seen more business casual than a corporate retreat. The couch is now an official meeting attendee.

Home office: where 'business in the front, party in the back' takes on a whole new meaning.

Working from home: where every day is casual Friday and the fridge is the new water cooler.

Blend home and work with grace; remember, even your plants enjoy a change of scenery.

EMAILS BREED OVERNIGHT IN MY INBOX. IT'S LIKE A DIGITAL BUNNY FARM WITHOUT THE CUTENESS.

EMAILS ARE LIKE BOOMERANGS; JUST WHEN YOU THINK YOU'VE THROWN THEM AWAY, THEY COME BACK.

Emails:
modern-day pigeons that never get lost on their way back.

Conquer your inbox with the tenacity of a hero in an epic saga—slay the spam dragon.

ON TODAY'S VIDEO CALL, MY CAT WAS THE ONLY ONE WHO AGREED WITH MY POINT. PURR-FECT CONSENSUS.

I've been on so many video calls, I accidentally tried to mute my family at dinner.

VIDEO CALLS: WHERE 'SORRY, YOU GO FIRST' IS THE NEW NATIONAL ANTHEM.

Embrace the chaos of video calls; sometimes, the best ideas come through in a cat cameo.

**Lunch break?
Oh, you mean that time I eat with one hand and type with the other?**

*Remember lunch breaks?
They're now historical fiction.*

**Lunch breaks:
A legend told by old-timers who saw the sun midday.**

Reclaim the mythical lunch break. Your creativity needs food as much as your stomach.

MY MULTITASKING IS SO ADVANCED, I CAN PROCRASTINATE ON SEVERAL TASKS SIMULTANEOUSLY.

I'm not juggling tasks; I'm playing hot potato with deadlines.

MULTITASKING: THE ART OF MESSING UP SEVERAL THINGS AT ONCE, BUT WITH FLAIR.

MASTER THE JUGGLE, BUT DON'T FORGET TO DROP THE BALL ON PURPOSE SOMETIMES. REST IS A TASK TOO.

AFTER WORK, I PLAN TO BE PRODUCTIVE. INSTEAD, MY COUCH AND I BOND OVER MUTUAL INACTIVITY.

AFTER WORK IS A MYTH, LIKE UNICORNS OR COMFORTABLE OFFICE CHAIRS.

AFTER-WORK PLANS ARE LIKE GYM MEMBERSHIPS:
GOOD INTENTIONS THAT RARELY SEE ACTION.

Chase the after-work mirage. Sometimes, it leads to an oasis of rest.

Vacation: that time I switch from emailing at my desk to emailing with a view.

I NEED A VACATION FROM PLANNING MY VACATION. THERE'S A SPREADSHEET INVOLVED.

Vacations: when you realize your full-time job is avoiding out-of-office guilt.

TAKE YOUR VACATION SERIOUSLY; IT'S THE ONLY JOB WHERE DOING NOTHING IS THE GOAL.

4.
ENVIRONMENTAL CONCERNS

I've sorted my recycling so many times, I feel like a contestant on 'The Sorting Hat's Got Talent'.

WHY DID THE RECYCLING BIN BREAK UP WITH THE TRASH CAN? IT COULDN'T HANDLE THE GARBAGE LIFESTYLE ANYMORE.

RECYCLING: WHERE YOU GET TO BE A WIZARD, TURNING TRASH INTO TREASURE. ABRACADABRA, PLASTIC BOTTLE BECOME PARK BENCH!

Keep calm and recycle on. Your trash could be another's treasure.

I BOUGHT A REUSABLE BAG THAT CAME IN THREE LAYERS OF PLASTIC PACKAGING.
I THINK THE IRONY WAS ALSO WRAPPED SEPARATELY.

Plastics have a 1000-year lifespan. Finally, something that's more committed than my ex.

PLASTIC BAGS ARE THE COCKROACHES OF THE CONSUMER WORLD; THEY REFUSE TO DIE.

EVERY PLASTIC BOTTLE YOU REFUSE REWRITES THE OCEAN'S FUTURE. CHOOSE WISELY.

CITY PARKS ARE SO SCARCE, MY DOG THINKS A FIRE HYDRANT IS A TREE. URBAN JUNGLE INDEED.

IF CONCRETE WAS A PLANT, CITIES WOULD BE THE RAINFORESTS OF HUMAN CIVILIZATION.

An urban jungle is where the wild things are... mostly squirrels with attitude and pigeons plotting rebellion.

GROW WHERE YOU ARE PLANTED, EVEN IF IT'S CONCRETE. GREEN UP YOUR URBAN SPACE.

MY TAP DRIPS WITH SUCH RHYTHM, IT'S LIKE HAVING A WATER-SAVING REMINDER WITH A BEAT.

WATER CONSERVATION IS IMPORTANT, BUT MY SHOWER CONCERTS JUST GOT A BAD REVIEW FROM THE DROUGHT COMMITTEE.

Saving water is like saving money; both drip away when you're not paying attention.

TURN OFF THE TAP WHILE BRUSHING. YOUR FUTURE SELF, PAYING WATER BILLS, WILL THANK YOU.

SWITCHED TO SOLAR POWER AND NOW MY HOUSE RUNS ON DAYLIGHT SAVINGS. LITERALLY.

RENEWABLE ENERGY IS GREAT UNTIL YOUR SOLAR-POWERED HOUSE STARTS FOLLOWING THE SUN LIKE A SUNFLOWER.

Solar panels: because the sun doesn't send you a utility bill.

EMBRACE CLEAN ENERGY; LET'S MAKE FOSSIL FUELS A THING OF THE DINOSAURS.

MY 'ECO-FRIENDLY' SHIRT CAME WITH A TAG, 'BEST BEFORE: NEXT FASHION SEASON'. FAST FASHION, INDEED.

FAST FASHION MOVES SO QUICKLY, BY THE TIME YOU WEAR IT, IT'S ALREADY OUT OF STYLE.

Fast fashion is like fast food: cheap, satisfying, and you always regret it later.

INVEST IN TIMELESS PIECES. LET FASHION SLOW DANCE, NOT SPRINT.

IN THE CITY, GREEN SPACE IS SO RARE, I SAW A KID TRYING TO CLIMB A PAINTED TREE.

I JOINED THE RACE FOR MORE GREEN SPACES.
IT'S LIKE 'THE AMAZING RACE', BUT EVERYONE'S A TURTLE.

Fighting for green spaces in the city is like playing musical chairs, nature edition.

CHAMPION GREEN SPACES;
EVEN A SINGLE TREE ADDS A VERSE TO THE URBAN SYMPHONY.

5.
ECONOMIC PRESSURE

THIS MONTH, MY BUDGETING SKILLS TURNED MY FINANCES FROM 'TITANIC' INTO 'LIFE OF PI'—I'M ON A TINY BOAT, BUT AT LEAST I'M AFLOAT.

MY BUDGETING APP BROKE UP WITH ME—SAID IT NEEDED SPACE.

Budgets are like diet plans for your wallet—mostly good intentions and creative excuses.

NAVIGATE YOUR BUDGET WITH THE SKILL OF A PIRATE—TREASURE WHAT MATTERS, AND DON'T BE AFRAID TO SAIL UNCHARTED WATERS.

Today, I was so into coupon clipping that I accidentally tried to redeem one at a family dinner.

I'M NOT SAYING I'M OBSESSED WITH COUPONS, BUT IF THERE WERE A COUPON FOR THERAPY, I'D DEFINITELY USE IT.

In the kingdom of budgeting, coupons are the loyal knights—valiant, but they sometimes miss the mark.

ARM YOURSELF WITH COUPONS. THE BATTLE FOR SAVINGS IS WON ONE SNIP AT A TIME.

As a freelancer, my job description includes CEO, accountant, and office janitor—multitasking at its finest.

Told my plants I'm freelancing. Now, they look at me for sunlight.

FREELANCING IS LIKE JUGGLING EGGS; DROP ONE, AND THINGS GET MESSY FAST.

IN THE CIRCUS OF FREELANCING, EVERY ACT IS YOUR SHOW. MAKE IT UNFORGETTABLE.

Navigating my mortgage felt like playing Monopoly with real money—terrifying and somewhat exhilarating.

Mortgages are like gym memberships—exciting at first, then you realize there's a lot of work involved.

A mortgage is just a fancy word for a financial marathon with a surprise finish line.

Treat your mortgage like a dragon to be tamed, not a monster to be feared.

Saving money in this economy is like keeping a chocolate bar intact on a hot day—almost impossible.

I started a savings account for emergencies. Found out pizza is an emergency.

SAVING MONEY IS LIKE A GAME OF TETRIS—JUST WHEN YOU THINK YOU'VE GOT IT SORTED, THE EXPENSES PILE UP AGAIN.

Build your savings brick by brick; even the Great Wall started as a single stone.

My investment strategy is like my approach to cooking—sometimes it's delicious, sometimes I'm just glad I survived.

INVESTING MONEY IS A LOT LIKE PLANTING TREES. YOU NEVER KNOW WHICH WILL GROW, BUT YOU HOPE IT'S NOT JUST THE WEEDS.

INVESTING: WHERE YOUR MONEY TAKES A ROLLERCOASTER RIDE, AND YOU'RE NOT TALL ENOUGH FOR THE RIDE.

NAVIGATE THE INVESTMENT JUNGLE WITH THE WISDOM OF AN OWL AND THE COURAGE OF A LION. FORTUNE FAVORS THE BOLD—AND THE INFORMED.

Planning for retirement feels like trying to solve a Rubik's cube—every time I think I'm close, I realize I'm not.

RETIREMENT PLANNING? I'M MORE OF A 'HOPE THE LOTTERY FINALLY PAYS OFF' KIND OF PLANNER.

Retirement is like reaching the horizon. It's beautiful from afar, but a whole lot further than it looks.

AIM FOR RETIREMENT LIKE IT'S A DISTANT, BEAUTIFUL ISLAND. ROW HARD, AND ONE DAY, YOU'LL REACH ITS SHORES.

6.
POLITICAL POLARIZATION

Attended a political debate where the most agreed-upon motion was 'Can we break for lunch?

WHY DON'T POLITICAL DEBATES EVER SOLVE PUZZLES? BECAUSE EVERYONE STICKS TO THEIR OWN PIECE.

Political debates: where you find out who your friends really are, and how many you're left with.

LET'S AGREE TO DISAGREE, AND THEN AGREE TO LAUGH ABOUT IT.

VOTING FELT LIKE CHOOSING MY FAVORITE DISASTER MOVIE: EXCITING, BUT I'D RATHER WATCH FROM HOME.

WHY DID THE VOTE GO TO SCHOOL?
TO BECOME 'ELECT'-ORATE.

Voting: the adult version of choosing your own adventure book, but with more plot twists.

EXERCISE YOUR RIGHT TO VOTE, AND THEN EXERCISE YOUR RIGHT TO NOT TAKE IT ALL TOO SERIOUSLY.

TRYING TO UNDERSTAND NEW POLICIES IS LIKE READING INSTRUCTIONS IN A FOREIGN LANGUAGE.
I KNOW IT'S IMPORTANT, BUT GOOGLE TRANSLATE ISN'T HELPING.

Policies are like gym memberships. Everyone agrees they're good for you, but interpreting them is another workout.

Policies:
They say they're to simplify life, yet here I am, more confused than ever.

WHEN IN DOUBT, LAUGH AT THE COMPLEXITY OF POLICIES.
IT'S BETTER THAN CRYING.

POLITICAL CAMPAIGNS ARE THE SEASON WHERE MY TV BECOMES A REALITY SHOW PRODUCER, SPECIALIZING IN DRAMA.

WHY DID THE POLITICAL CAMPAIGN THROW A PARTY? BECAUSE THEY MASTERED THE ART OF SPIN-THE-BOTTLE.

Campaigns:
the only time when everyone suddenly cares about your opinion, while telling you theirs.

Enjoy the campaign season like a circus; appreciate the spectacle, but don't get lost in the tents.

Entered a political discussion online.
Came out an hour later, wondering if my cat could run for office.

**Social media:
where political careers go for a workout, and sometimes, a knockout.**

ONLINE POLITICAL DEBATES: PROOF THAT KEYBOARDS MIGHT BE MIGHTIER THAN SWORDS, BUT JUST AS DOUBLE-EDGED.

Dive into social media battles with humor as your shield.
It's the best armor.

SHARED MY POLITICAL OPINION AT DINNER. IT TURNED INTO A SPORT WHERE EVERYONE PLAYED, BUT NOBODY WON.

WHY DID THE OPINION GO TO THERAPY? BECAUSE IT WAS POLARIZED!

**Opinions in politics:
more abundant than popcorn at the movies, and just as likely to cause a mess.**

TREAT OPINIONS LIKE A MARATHON; PACE YOURSELF, AND REMEMBER, FINISHING IS BETTER THAN WINNING.

SAW A POLITICIAN PREACHING UNITY. FOR A MOMENT, WE ALL BELIEVED IN UNICORNS AGAIN.

Unity in politics is like a rare Pokémon. Everyone talks about it, but no one knows how to catch it.

UNITY IN POLITICS: THE MYTHICAL CREATURE WE ALL HOPE TO SEE, BUT SUSPECT IS JUST WEARING AN EXCELLENT DISGUISE.

Chase unity like the elusive creature it is; with hope, laughter, and a grain of salt.

7.
SOCIAL ISOLATION

Decided to social distance from my fridge.
Our relationship was getting too intense.

I'M NOT ALONE; I HAVE A HOUSEPLANT FOR COMPANY. WE'RE PLANNING A QUIET NIGHT IN.

Social isolation: when your web history knows more about your social life than your friends.

**EMBRACE SOLITUDE LIKE IT'S AN EXCLUSIVE PARTY FOR ONE.
DRESS CODE: PAJAMAS PREFERRED.**

Attended a virtual party and experienced buffering. Now I know what it feels like to be paused in real life.

Virtual hangouts: where 'Can you hear me?' is the new 'Cheers!'

Online parties: where you can be a wallflower and no one will know you're actually against a wall.

CONNECT DIGITALLY, BUT REMEMBER, NO SCREEN CAN REPLICATE A HUG.
VIRTUAL CHEERS TO REAL FEELINGS!

*Started singing in the shower as my daily social interaction.
My shampoo bottles are now my biggest fans.*

Karaoke night at my place involves singing duets solo. I play both parts expertly.

SINGING ALONE: THE ONLY TIME WHEN YOU'RE GUARANTEED TO BE IN PERFECT HARMONY WITH YOURSELF.

Let your solo serenades fill the silence. Music is the sound of feelings understood.

I've started talking to my furniture. The couch thinks I should see other people.

I WENT ON A QUEST FOR SILENCE. FOUND IT, BUT MISSED THE NOISE.

In the quest for quiet, I discovered my thoughts were the loudest guests at the party.

Seek solace in silence but listen for the echoes of laughter.
Solitude need not be silent.

Joined a book club for one. It's great; we always agree on the book.

My book club meets in my head. It's an exclusive gathering.

IN MY BOOK CLUB, WE SIP WINE, DEBATE CHARACTERS, AND PLOT TWISTS. ATTENDANCE: ME, MYSELF, AND I.

DIVE INTO STORIES AS IF THEY'RE SOCIAL EVENTS. EACH PAGE, A CONVERSATION; EVERY CHAPTER, A NEW FRIEND.

Cooked a meal for one and set the table for two. My appetite needed its own seat.

I talk to my pasta. It's the only thing that understands me al dente

Cooking for one: where the food is always good company, and the leftovers are a reminder of a feast well-enjoyed.

Let your meals be a companion. In every bite, a story; in every flavor, a memory.

Explored my apartment like it was a new continent. Discovered lost civilizations under my bed.

BECAME AN INDOOR EXPLORER. FOUND ANCIENT ARTIFACTS IN MY FRIDGE DATING BACK TO THE 'BEFORE TIMES

Indoor exploring: where you find treasures in forgotten drawers and adventures in unopened mail.

EMBARK ON INDOOR ADVENTURES.
EVERY NOOK A LANDMARK, EACH ROOM A NEW TERRAIN TO CONQUER.

8.

EDUCATION AND PARENTING

*Helped my kid with math homework.
Suddenly, 'new math' made me miss my old grades.*

HOMEWORK IS A TEST FOR PARENTS, AND LET ME TELL YOU, I'M NOT SCORING AN A.

HOMEWORK:
THE ULTIMATE TEST OF FAMILY HARMONY, ONE WORKSHEET AT A TIME.

Tackle homework with patience and chocolate.
The answers are sweeter that way.

INSTITUTED A SCREEN TIME LIMIT. MY KIDS BECAME NEGOTIATORS I DIDN'T KNOW I WAS RAISING.

Screen time limits are great for developing kids' bargaining skills.

SCREEN TIME: BECAUSE EVERY PARENT NEEDS A BREAK, EVEN IF IT'S JUST TO BLINK.

Balance screen time with dream time.
Let imagination, not just apps, fuel their play.

Mornings used to be coffee and quiet.
Now, it's cereal in my hair and a race against the clock.

Our family morning routine is a well-oiled machine—if that machine was designed by a toddler.

Morning madness: proving that chaos theory applies to families, especially before coffee.

Embrace the morning chaos; it's the soundtrack of a family alive with love and lost socks.

School drop-off is like a reality TV show: 'Survivor: The Parking Lot'.

Dropping my kids off at school requires the stealth of a ninja and the patience of a saint.

School drop-off: where you learn that 'quick goodbye' is an oxymoron.

TREASURE THE DROP-OFF DRAMA; ONE DAY, YOU'LL MISS BEING THEIR DAILY CHAUFFEUR.

AT THE PARENT-TEACHER CONFERENCE, I LEARNED MORE ABOUT MYSELF THAN I DID ABOUT MY CHILD.

Parent-teacher conferences: confirming that my child is indeed my mini-me.

PARENT-TEACHER MEETINGS: WHERE YOU FIND OUT YOUR APPLE DIDN'T FALL FAR FROM THE TREE, AND NOW IT'S HOMEWORK'S TURN.

Approach parent-teacher conferences as a team huddle.
Together, you're unstoppable.

SIGNED THE KIDS UP FOR ONE TOO MANY ACTIVITIES.
OUR CALENDAR NOW LOOKS LIKE A TETRIS GAME.

I DON'T HAVE HOBBIES ANYMORE; I HAVE CHILDREN'S EXTRACURRICULAR ACTIVITIES.

EXTRACURRICULARS: BECAUSE WHO NEEDS FREE TIME WHEN YOU CAN HAVE A FULL ITINERARY BEFORE AGE 10?

Foster passions, not schedules. Let them find their joy, not just their next appointment.

BEDTIME IS WHEN MY KIDS SUDDENLY REMEMBER ALL THEIR LIFE'S AMBITIONS AND EXISTENTIAL QUESTIONS.

My kids treat bedtime like a suggestion, not a rule.

Bedtime:
That magical time when children morph into thirsty philosophers with unfinished novels.

Cherish the bedtime battles.
One day, they'll sleep before you even say 'goodnight.'

9.
CULTURAL SHIFTS

Remember when 'tweeting' was for birds?
Now, my grandma has more followers than a small country

Social media: where everyone's meal looks better than mine. Guess I missed the 'filter' on my stove.

NAVIGATING SOCIAL MEDIA IS LIKE ATTENDING A MASQUERADE BALL. EVERYONE'S MASKED, BUT THE PARTY'S TOO LOUD TO IGNORE.

Embrace the digital dance, but don't forget the music of real-life conversations.

With so many streaming services, my TV is more cultured than I am. Last week, it took a virtual trip to Paris.

I ASKED MY TV FOR A MOVIE RECOMMENDATION.
IT SUGGESTED I GO OUTSIDE.

Streaming: Turning 'just one more episode' into a cultural phenomenon and personal challenge.

Dive into the streaming sea, but remember to come up for air and real-world adventures.

Saw a teen wearing clothes from my high school years calling it 'vintage.' Suddenly felt both old and trendy.

RETRO FASHION IS BACK. SAVED ME A FORTUNE ON A NEW WARDROBE—I JUST RAIDED MY ATTIC.

Fashion is a boomerang; what you threw out in disgust will hit you back in vogue.

WEAR YOUR YEARS WITH PRIDE; EVERY TREND HAS ITS DAY, INCLUDING THE ONES WE LIVED THROUGH.

Gourmet coffee shops are on every corner. My espresso has more passport stamps than I do.

I'm not a foodie.
I'm a flavor explorer on a journey where every meal is a new destination.

THE FOODIE REVOLUTION: MAKING 'WHAT'S FOR DINNER?' THE MOST COMPLEX QUESTION OF THE DAY.

SAVOR THE WORLD ONE BITE AT A TIME, BUT DON'T FORGET THE SIMPLE JOY OF HOME-COOKED MEALS.

MY OFFICE IS NOW WHEREVER MY LAPTOP OPENS. LAST WEEK, IT WAS A BEACH. TODAY, MY SOFA. PRODUCTIVITY, OR LACK THEREOF, FOLLOWS.

**TOLD MY BOSS I'M EMBRACING THE 'WORK FROM ANYWHERE' POLICY.
CURRENTLY, THE LOCATION IS 'DENIAL.'**

The 'work from anywhere' era: Blurring the lines between 'home office' and 'I live at work.'

FIND YOUR ANYWHERE,
BUT ANCHOR YOUR SOMEWHERE.
BALANCE IS KEY,
EVEN WHEN YOUR OFFICE HAS A SEA VIEW.

*Bought a reusable straw.
I've saved the oceans
but can't find the straw.*

JOINING THE GREEN MOVEMENT.
I'M NOT JUST RECYCLING JOKES;
I'M COMPOSTING THEM
FOR BETTER USE.

THE GREEN MOVEMENT:
WHERE YOU'RE NOT SURE IF
YOU'RE SAVING THE PLANET OR
JUST COLLECTING MORE BINS.

**Every small green step counts.
Even if it's just rescuing your
reusable straw from under the car
seat.**

WENT OFFLINE FOR A DETOX.
FOUND OUT THERE'S A REAL WORLD
OUT THERE, NOT JUST HD.

**Digital detox:
It's like a juice cleanse, but the headaches
are from withdrawal, not hunger.**

DIGITAL DETOX:
REDISCOVERING LIFE'S ANALOG
PLEASURES,
LIKE TALKING TO PLANTS OR
READING PAPER BOOKS.

Unplug to recharge.
Your best connections aren't
measured in bars or likes.

10.

PERSONAL IDENTITY AND SELF-EXPRESSION

Decided my wardrobe needed a makeover.
Now, it's less 'fashion-forward' and more 'time-traveler chic'

MY SOCKS NEVER MATCH. I CALL IT 'CREATIVE EXPRESSION', MY MOM CALLS IT 'LAUNDRY DAY'.

PERSONAL STYLE IS JUST YOUR SOCIAL MEDIA PROFILE IN 3D: CURATED, COLORFUL, AND SOMETIMES CONFUSING.

WEAR YOUR IDENTITY LIKE A BADGE OF HONOR. IF IT'S COMFORTABLE, IT'S YOU

PICKED UP A NEW HOBBY EVERY MONTH LAST YEAR.
MY LIVING ROOM NOW LOOKS LIKE A CRAFT STORE EXPLODED.

I HAVE TWO HOBBIES: COLLECTING HOBBIES AND THEN ABANDONING THEM FOR NEW ONES.

Hobbies are the fingerprints of the soul. Unique, messy, and often overlapping.

Embrace every hobby. Each one adds a layer to your identity, like paint on a masterpiece.

MY ONLINE PERSONA IS SO POLISHED, I SOMETIMES NEED TO REMIND MYSELF WHAT I ACTUALLY LIKE.

ONLINE, I'M AN ADVENTURER, A POET, AND A CHEF. OFFLINE, I'M CONFUSED BY THE TOASTER.

OUR DIGITAL SELVES ARE LIKE AVATARS IN A GAME WHERE WE FORGOT WE'RE THE PLAYERS, NOT THE CHARACTERS.

Craft your digital persona with care, but let your real self play the lead role.

LEARNED THREE PHRASES
IN A NEW LANGUAGE:
'HELLO,' 'GOODBYE,' AND 'WHERE'S THE
BATHROOM?'
I'M PRACTICALLY FLUENT.

My body language speaks volumes.
It's mostly saying, 'I need more coffee.'

THE LANGUAGE OF SELF IS
UNIVERSAL, YET DEEPLY PERSONAL.
SOMETIMES IT'S IN THE SILENCE
BETWEEN WORDS.

Speak your truth, in whatever
language it comes.
Authenticity needs no translation.

*Embraced my flaws and now we're having a party.
Turns out, they're fantastic company.*

I'M PERFECTLY IMPERFECT. WHICH MEANS I'M DOING SOMETHING RIGHT, JUST NOT CONSISTENTLY.

**Imperfection:
the signature of authenticity on the artwork of our souls.**

CELEBRATE YOUR IMPERFECTIONS; THEY'RE THE BRUSHSTROKES OF YOUR UNIQUE MASTERPIECE.

SEARCHED FOR MY 'AUTHENTIC SELF.'
FOUND IT HIDING IN THE LAST PLACE
I LEFT IT:
BETWEEN DREAMS AND LAUGHTER.

My quest for authenticity led me to the fridge. Turns out, I'm genuinely hungry.

Authenticity is a journey with pit stops in doubt, detours through reflection, and scenic routes through joy.

Be fearlessly authentic. The world craves originality, and you're it.

Looking back, I've changed so much I could introduce myself to my past self. We'd have lots to catch up on.

I'M NOT WHO I WAS A YEAR AGO, WHICH IS GREAT BECAUSE I'VE FORGOTTEN SOME OF THEIR PASSWORDS.

OUR PERSONAL EVOLUTION IS THE ONLY SERIES WORTH BINGE-WATCHING.
SPOILER ALERT:
THE PROTAGONIST TRIUMPHS.

Embrace your evolution.
Every version of you
is a season in the epic series of
'Being Myself.'

11.

FUTURE UNCERTAINTY

Asked a fortune teller about my future.
She said to check back tomorrow.

I'M CERTAIN ABOUT FUTURE UNCERTAINTY.
IT'S THE ONE CONSTANT PREDICTION.

The future is like a surprise party planned by the universe.
You know it's coming;
you just don't know what to expect.

***EMBRACE THE MYSTERY OF TOMORROW.
IT KEEPS LIFE INTERESTING.***

My career path looks less like a ladder and more like a game of Chutes and Ladders.

THINKING OF A CAREER IN TIME TRAVEL.
I HEAR THERE'S NO FUTURE IN IT.

CHOOSING A CAREER IS LIKE PICKING A STREAMING SERVICE.
NO MATTER WHAT YOU CHOOSE, YOU WONDER WHAT YOU'RE MISSING.

NAVIGATE YOUR CAREER WITH FLEXIBILITY.
IT'S ABOUT THE JOURNEY, NOT JUST THE DESTINATION.

DATING NOWADAYS IS LIKE GAMBLING.
MOST TIMES, IT'S A RISK, BUT YOU MIGHT HIT THE JACKPOT.

**I TOLD MY DATE I WANTED A STABLE RELATIONSHIP.
NOW WE'RE BOTH TAKING HORSEBACK RIDING LESSONS.**

Modern relationships: where 'It's complicated' is the most common status update.

Cherish connections, roll with the changes, and remember, laughter is the best icebreaker.

Bought the latest gadget. By the time I figured it out, it was obsolete.

IN THE FUTURE, TECHNOLOGY WILL DO EVERYTHING FOR US. CAN'T WAIT TO BE UNEMPLOYED BY A TOASTER.

Technology's promise: to make life easier, one incomprehensible user manual at a time.

Adapt to new tech with curiosity. After all, today's magic is tomorrow's tweet.

Investing in the stock market with the hope it's like my plants: grows with minimal attention.

MY FINANCIAL PLAN IS TO HOPE FOR THE BEST.
AND MAYBE BUY A LOTTERY TICKET.

ECONOMIC FORECASTS PREDICT EVERYTHING BUT THEIR OWN ACCURACY.

*Plan for the future with optimism.
And always have a piggy bank as plan B.*

Joined a gym to get in shape for the future.
So far, my future's looking... round.

IN THE FUTURE, WE'LL ALL BE FIT FROM JUMPING TO CONCLUSIONS.

THE FUTURE OF HEALTH: WHERE WE'RE ALL JUST ONE APP AWAY FROM BECOMING A VERSION OF OURSELVES THAT DOESN'T LIKE SITTING.

INVEST IN YOUR HEALTH LIKE IT'S A RETIREMENT PLAN.
THE BEST WEALTH IS HEALTH.

THE ENVIRONMENT'S FUTURE
IS SO UNCERTAIN,
MY PLASTIC BOTTLES ARE
HAVING AN EXISTENTIAL CRISIS.

Future environmental plan:
convince aliens to adopt us and our planet.

Tomorrow's weather forecast:
partly cloudy with a chance of
climate change.

TREAT THE PLANET LIKE A
LEGACY.
LET'S ENSURE THE FUTURE IS
NOT JUST SUSTAINABLE BUT
THRIVING.

12.

INFORMATION OVERLOAD

TRIED KEEPING UP WITH THE NEWS.
NOW, I'M DIZZY FROM THE SPIN CYCLE.

Why did the news go to therapy?
It had too many issues.

In the whirlpool of information, staying afloat means knowing when to swim and when to float.

FILTER YOUR NEWS LIKE COFFEE;
LET THE GROUNDS SETTLE
BEFORE TAKING A SIP.

SOCIAL MEDIA IS MY DAILY FLOOD.
I'M BUILDING AN ARK.

SOCIAL MEDIA:
WHERE EVERYONE'S LIFE IS A BLOCKBUSTER, AND MINE'S A BLOOPER REEL.

Drowning in social media? Remember, even Noah had to choose what to let on the ark.

Navigate the flood of posts with a paddle of perspective.
It's okay to sail past most.

Opened my inbox and found an email tsunami.
My delete key is now a lifeboat.

MY INBOX IS LIKE A GAME OF TETRIS.
NO MATTER HOW FAST
I CLEAR IT,
THE EMAILS PILE UP QUICKER.

EMAILS:
THE ONLY FLOOD WHERE YOU DROWN IN WHAT YOU DON'T SEE.

In the sea of emails, be the lighthouse, not the buoy.
Shine a light on what matters.

DOWNLOADED SO MANY APPS, MY PHONE'S NOW AN AVALANCHE RISK.

There's an app for everything.
I'm waiting for the one that stops
me from downloading more apps.

*APPS:
WHERE 'THERE'S ONE FOR THAT' TURNS
INTO 'THERE'S TOO MUCH OF THAT.*

TREAD CAREFULLY THROUGH
THE APP AVALANCHE.
THE RIGHT TOOLS SHOULD
LIBERATE, NOT BURY YOU.

ONLINE SHOPPING IS LIKE A BOX OF CHOCOLATES.
YOU NEVER KNOW WHAT YOU'RE GONNA GET, BUT THE BILL IS ALWAYS A SURPRISE.

I accidentally hit 'buy now' instead of 'cancel.'
Guess I'm committed to this relationship now.

In the supermarket of the internet, every aisle is a temptation and every click adds to the cart.

SHOP WITH INTENTION, NOT IMPULSE. YOUR SPACE, LIKE YOUR MIND, APPRECIATES THE EXTRA ROOM.

Tried a digital detox.
It was great until I realized I was talking to a plant... and it didn't reply.

Digital detox is the new diet. You crave everything you can't have, especially the likes.

Digital detox:
Because sometimes, the best connection is reconnection—with the offline world.

Unplug to recharge.
Your best connections are not Wi-Fi dependent.

Decided to learn online.
It's a curve alright, more like a loop.
I keep starting over.

Online learning: where you're always a student, especially of patience.

THE INTERNET'S LEARNING CURVE IS LESS A CURVE AND MORE A SPIRAL—ENTERTAINING, BUT DIZZYING.

Embrace the vast classroom of the internet, but remember, the teacher is in the pause, not the scroll.

www.ingramcontent.com/pod-product-compliance
Lightning Source LLC
Chambersburg PA
CBHW071021080526
44587CB00015B/2447